One Prompt a
Day for young
Adults
Belongs to

____

Aldona Design

Date________________________
What's are you looking Forward to today?

Date_____________________

What made you smile today

Date________________________
Your past Achievement

Date__________________

What are you grateful for

Date_____________________

What is your best meal of the day?

Date________________________

The last book you read

Date________________
What brings you Happiness ?

Date______________________

The best ice cream flavour

Date________________
Your goal for today

Date________________________

Complete the sentence, I enjoy .....

Date____________________
Your favourite Music Artist

Date_______________________
The new thing you like to learn

Date_______________
Did you keep up to your resolution

Date_____________________
Your best time of the day

Date________________________

The Dish I enjoy the most

Date________________________

Best month of the year

Date________________

Habits to avoid...

Date________________
Skills need to work on

Date_______________________

Habits to fix

Date___________________
Name the person you cannot do without

Date__________________

Goals to achieve by the end of next month

Date________________________

Best day of your life

Date________________________
The dish you like to prepare

Date______________________

Daily motivation

Date____________________
Fashion Style

Date______________________

Who inspires you the most

Date________________________

Best season of the year!

Date______________________

The past makes you.......

Date_________________
The present......

Date_______________________

Travel plans

Date_______________________

What brings good memories ?

Date______________________

Reminders for the month

Date________________________

Savings for last month

Date_________________

The gifts that brings you joy

Date_______________________

Best movie you've seen

Date__________________

Food you have still to try

Date________________

Best restaurant...

Date______________________

Sports you play

Date________________________

Child hood days.....,

Date________________
Looking forward to...

Date_____________________
Best outfit......

Date_________________

Country to visit

Date________________
Rainy days are.....

Date____________________
Summer can ......,

Date________________________

Date______________________

Your best winter Activity

Date______________________
What made you laugh this week

Date______________________

The joke that still makes you laugh

Date________________
Best Day of the week & Why

Date________________

Favourite Colour

Date________________
Last Expensive shopping made you.....

Date________________
When was the last foolish thing you did

Date_______________________

Little things bring pleasure what are those to you

Date________________
Best year of your life

Date________________
The thing you should do more often

Date________________________

Best days of your life

Date______________________

Date_______________________

Dull cloudy days brings...

Date______________________

Your best buddy

Date_________________
Sunshine keeps you.....

Date________________

Feelings of today

Date________________
What keeps you motivated

Date________________________

The best part of today

Date________________________

The task to be completed...

Date________________________

Your best daily routine

Date_____________________
What Kind deeds you did for your friend

Date__________________
Best time of the year

Date______________________

Habits to change

Date_____________________
Your feelings of today

Date_______________________

Best TV Serial you've watched

Date________________
The celebration I enjoyed

Date________________
The companion that keeps you happy

Date________________________
Greenery makes you

Date________________________

Blessings in your life

Date________________

The best fun day

Date_______________________

Busy days of the year...

Date________________
The person your thankful to

Date______________________

Who makes you laugh

Date________________
Your present job

Date________________
Who is your role model

Date________________________
Amount of water intake

Date________________

Overall health is

Date________________________

I need to fix.....

Date____________________
I have learnt to..........

Date_______________________

Best fitness routine

Date______________________

Memories of School days

Date____________________

What you liked about this Month?

Date_______________________

Saying No makes you ...

Date________________________

Saying yes when you want to say no
/ What you think

Date________________________

Cheapest gift you gave to

Date______________________
Funny things you did last month

Date_______________________
I always forget to.....

Date________________

The person your grateful for

Date_________________________

Seeing is believing, do you agree

Date________________
Your Best Quote

Date________________________
Memories of Your last birthday celebration

Date_______________________

The things you did one step at a time

Date_______________________

Flowers is it the best gift

Date_____________________

Baking makes me....

Date_______________________

Best household chores

Date_____________________

Prayer for the month

Date______________________

The person you admire the most

Date________________________

What is it that makes you anxious?

Date_________________

The best part of dinning out

Date________________________
What food makes you hangry for more?

Date______________________
I walk away from......

Date________________
Stay connected with...,

Date________________________

Autumn brings feeling of

Date_______________________
The vegetable you haven't eaten

Date____________________

The last donation you have given

Date________________________

Lesson you learnt

Date_____________________

Holidays you wont forget

Date________________

What in abundance do you own ?

Date_______________________

What surprises you the most ?

Date_______________________

I cant get away with..,.,.

Date____________________

Your best drink

Date________________
How was your last weekend ?

Date_____________________

Sunday is it fun day!

Date_______________

After a hectic day, you relax with..

Date____________________

Reminders for the Day

Date______________________

Shopping makes me

Date________________

What's your best breakfast

Date________________________

If you had to skip a meal which would it be ?

Date________________
You cannot do without……

Date________________

What you eat on a hectic day !

Date____________________

Best Game to watch.....

Date________________________

What keeps you busy on weekends?

Date_______________________

Your best outfit that makes you comfortable

Date________________________

If you had to invent something, What would it be

Date__________________
If you had to go camping, who would you
exclude?

Date____________________

Would you prefer walking uphill or downhill ?

Date________________
Best adventure

Date________________________
Robots is it necessary !

Date________________

What makes it a fruitful day

Date____________________
Happy conversation you had recently

Date______________________

Which was the best years of your life

Date_______________________

Favourite Animal and why?

Date_____________________

How do you overcome fears?

Date_____________________
What makes a perfect meal!

Date____________________

Its got to be perfect, What is it

Date________________________

Best mystery book you've read

Date________________________

When was the last time, you participated in a
fundraising

Date________________________
Who did you go shopping with ?

Date____________________

The advice you cherish that you got from your grand parents

Date________________
What gets you Excited ?

Date_________________________

What seems funny to you?

Date______________________

When did you last say Thankyou?

Date________________

When did you last say I love you ?

Date________________________

Your morning routine on week days

Date________________________

Have you Achieved anything from writing
an answer to these prompts,
Also don't Forget to write a review about
This book   link below

www.amazon.com/author/aldonadesign

Thank You

List of other books on Amazon By

Aldona Design

Blank ruled Zodiac notebooks designed
- **Pisces**
- **Taurus**
- **Leo**
- **Gemini**
- **others still to be published**
- **Music Manuscript notebook**
- **Planners For Hairstylist, Dentist,**
- **Planners for mum, Dad**
- **Planners for Graduates**
- **Weekly Meal Plans**
- **My Juice Diet**
- **My own Nail art Design**
- **Colouring books for adults**
- **Work Books for children**
- **Printed patterned paper (For DIY)**
- **Book of Gift tags**

www.amazon.com/author/aldonadesign

www.ingramcontent.com/pod-product-compliance
Lightning Source LLC
Chambersburg PA
CBHW061348250726
48657CB00004B/1384